YOUR FIRST COACHING BOOK

A Practical Guide for Volunteer Coaches

Cover Designer: Phaedra Mastrocola
In-House Editor: Marie Caratozzolo
Typesetter: Gary A. Rosenberg

Square One Publishers
Garden City Park, New York 11040
www.squareonepublishers.com

Library of Congress Cataloging-in-Publication Data
Your first coaching book : a practical guide for volunteer coaches / the
National Alliance For Youth Sports.
    p. cm.
Includes index.
   ISBN 0-7570-0200-5
  1. Sports for children—Coaching. I. National Alliance For Youth Sports.
   GV709.24 .Y68 2002
   796'.07'7—dc21

                         2002005192

Printed in the United States of America

10   9   8   7   6   5   4   3   2   1

CONTENTS

To the countless dedicated recreation professionals,
volunteer coaches, parents, and league administrators
who are involved in youth sports, and whose mission
is to ensure a safe, positive sports experience
for all children.

ACKNOWLEDGMENTS

This book is the culmination of over twenty years of interviews with volunteer coaches, league administrators, and parents who are involved in children's sports. In addition, it includes advice from hundreds of recreation professionals, who, through their loyalty to the goals of the National Alliance For Youth Sports, have provided the guidance and encouragement to keep sports positive and safe for all of America's youth. We gratefully acknowledge these dedicated individuals.

Credit must also be given to Greg Bach, the Communications Director for the Alliance, for his role in the creation of *Your First Coaching Book*. Greg is responsible for taking the information gathered over the years and crafting it into an easy-flowing, comprehensive, easy-to-read format. His reader-friendly writing style will be appreciated by first-time coaches as well as experienced veterans.

INTRODUCTION

There are few things in life more rewarding than coaching a youth sports team. It doesn't matter if you've stepped forward because you want to be actively involved with your son or daughter this season, or if you were somehow persuaded by the innocent-looking woman at the registration desk, who pleaded that the league was in desperate need of coaches and that you'd be perfect.

Regardless of why you volunteered, one thing is certain—you are about to embark on a wonderful journey filled with special moments that you will carry forever. You'll be there to congratulate your young players when they get their first hit or grab a game-winning touchdown pass. You'll also be the one to console them and bolster their spirits when they miss the crucial free throw that could have won the game. You'll emphasize good sportsmanship and playing by the rules. You'll preach the merits of teamwork, effort, and commitment. They'll call you "Coach," but you'll be so much more. You'll be a teacher, role model, friend, confidant, disciplinarian, and the mother or father figure for some.

It will be an amazing experience, but not necessarily an easy one. After all, you will have a group of youngsters under your supervision for an entire season. You'll also have their parents, grandparents, friends, and neighbors, who will be watching, examining, and dissecting your every move. You'll probably see your fair share of win-at-all-costs coaches who are intent on proving that their team is better than yours, and that they're better than you, even if it is a T-ball league of five-year olds who aren't any bigger than the bats they're swinging. Yes, youth sports can be a pretty intriguing mixture of experiences.

If you venture into the season unprepared, the role of coach can be a frustrating one. Enter *Your First Coaching Book*. Designed specifically for the volunteer coach, this handy resource will help you deal with a variety of issues you are likely to face at some point during the season. Part of a series of books developed by the National Alliance For Youth Sports—America's leading advocate for positive and safe sports for children—this book offers lots of helpful tips and useful advice to help ensure a fun-filled season for you, the parents, and most important, the youngsters on your team.

It doesn't matter if you're coaching a six-year-old girls soccer team or a group of fifteen-year-old football players. In either case, you're likely to face a variety of challenges, and this book extends a hand to help you deal with them. You'll learn how to effectively communicate with youngsters who have vastly different personalities, backgrounds, talents, and skill levels, and mold them into a cohesive, spirited team. You'll discover how to design effective practices that encourage your players to develop basic skills while boosting their self-esteem. You'll also learn valuable methods for dealing with meddling parents and volatile coaches, as well as children with short attention spans and bad attitudes. You'll recognize and understand the challenges that many coaches encounter, and gain confidence in knowing how to handle them.

Regardless if you're a first-year coach or a veteran who has taken countless post-game trips to the local ice cream parlor, coaching young children is drastically different from coaching on the high school, college, or professional level. How you handle the youngsters on your team and the way you interact with them at practices and games will have an enormous impact on whether or not they embrace the sport. Reflect on your own experience. You'll probably remember the names of most of your coaches, and whether or not your experience was fun. A coach's influence can have a lasting impression on children. Keep this thought in mind each time you step onto a field, court, or rink with your players.

The kids on your team will be putting their trust in you. They'll count on you to guide, teach, and motivate them. They'll be looking to you for a smile and a high-five when they do something well, and a pat on the back or a word of encouragement when things don't go their way. These children are going to remember you for the rest of their lives, and the experiences they have with you will be forever etched into their memories. *Your First Coaching Book* is a valuable resource to ensure that their memories are happy ones.

1. What Every Coach Should Know

Coaching youth sports these days involves a lot more than just showing up with a whistle, a clipboard, and a bag of equipment. It takes more than a practice plan that you've thrown together while sitting at a red light on the drive over. If you've never coached a youth sports team before, the responsibilities and demands may seem a little daunting at first. After all, you've got rules to digest, practices to schedule, and plays to orchestrate. You have youngsters to communicate with, parents to contend with, and other coaches to get along with. What does every coach need to know? Let's take a look at some of the basics.

UNDERSTAND THE GOALS OF THE LEAGUE

Do you really know what you got yourself into this season? When the league director persuaded you to take over a team, did he mention that it was an elite travel team that will be competing in weekend tournaments that are held throughout the state all summer long? Relax. It isn't likely that you'll be assigned such an advanced team. If you're coaching for the first time, you will probably be placed with a regular team that has a limited practice schedule and will be playing one or two local games a week.

Although the example regarding the travel team may be a bit extreme, it makes a point—always have a clear understanding of what your job involves. Know the competitiveness of the league and the playing abilities of the youngsters before making any commitments. Certainly, if you've never coached before, you probably won't be comfortable getting involved in a highly competitive league where winning is the top priority.

Understand the league's philosophy and know its focus. How closely does it match your own? Does it encourage equal playing time for everyone? Is it modeled after professional leagues with tryouts and drafts? Does it require the coaches to go through training or some type of certification program? Does it insist that the players wear available safety equipment? Be sure the philosophy of the league is in direct agreement with what is important to you as a coach.

DEVELOP YOUR OWN COACHING PHILOSOPHY

The philosophy of every volunteer coach should be centered around fun and good sportsmanship. It should encourage building each player's self-esteem. Certainly sounds simple enough, but you'd be surprised at how hard this can be to maintain. Good intentions are often discarded once the season begins and scoreboards, league standings, and championship trophies enter the picture.

From your very first contact with the team, your primary goal should be to maintain an atmosphere that tells the children they're going to have a lot of fun throughout the season. Make sure they understand that the number of wins doesn't matter—that it won't factor into the amount of fun they're going to have.

Another important goal of your coaching philosophy

should be to make each child feel that he or she is a valuable and contributing member of the team. Always focus on *all* of your kids, not just the ones who run faster, throw harder, or catch better. You've got to find a way to do this. If some of the players on your team reach their athletic potential, that's great; but it really takes a backseat to the children who come away from the experience feeling positive simply because they were part of the team—that they got the chance to play and, perhaps, made some progress with the skills of the sport.

Having and maintaining a positive philosophy that builds a child's self-esteem while encouraging fun and good sportsmanship should be your goal. It should be your coaching philosophy, which is discussed in greater detail in Chapter 4.

KNOW THE RULES OF THE SPORT

You won't find sports rulebooks on any bestseller list—and with good reason. They're pretty boring. But they *should* be at the top of every volunteer coach's required reading list.

You've got to become a student of the game and learn all the rules of the sport, as well as familiarize yourself with the particular rulebook the league is using. If you don't, there's no way the youngsters on your team can be expected to learn them either. And never assume that the players know all the rules, particularly for sports like baseball and basketball, where this assumption is typical.

Teaching the rules to your players is essential in the skill-development process. If they don't understand them and know how they're applied, it will be a frustrating experience for both you and them. Imagine how embarrassing it would be to question an official on a call regarding a rule that is clearly explained in your league's rulebook. Even if you have an extensive background in the sport and consider yourself knowledgeable, it's still strongly suggested to at least scan through a rulebook—give yourself a refresher—before getting started.

START WITH THE BASICS

One of the most important characteristics of a good coach is being able to teach. Good teaching means presenting information clearly and correctly, giving children time to practice, and offering them feedback on how well they perform. A good coach must be able to identify both efficient and inefficient performances, as well as analyze and correct any errors. Being able to do so will help your players develop those skills that are necessary to perform competitively.

Every sport requires certain essential skills. One of your jobs is to help your players develop them. To be too wrapped up in the Xs and Os of the game, determined that your players are going to execute intricate plays and elaborate strategies is unrealistic and counterproductive. Instead, stay focused on the basics. Begin with step one of a skill, making sure the child masters it before moving to the next, more challenging level. This is the most effective way to build their knowledge and skill of the sport, as well as their confidence and self-esteem.

For example, let's say you're coaching first- or second-year soccer players and trying to help them develop the skill of taking shots on goal. Start your players with a drill that involves the most basic component of this skill—kicking a stationary ball into an empty net. Encourage them to repeat this action until they do it well consistently. Next, increase the level of difficulty by adding motion to the drill—either roll the ball to the players and have them kick it toward the goal, or instruct them to run toward the stationary ball and kick it into the net. Once this step has been mastered, increase the challenge by adding a goaltender to stop the ball or a defender for the player to maneuver around before shooting.

Keep in mind the value of giving each player as many repetitions of a drill as possible to maximize practice time. While different players need to work on different skills, coaches typically do not have the luxury of being able to work one-on-one with each child due to time constraints. Consequently, it's important to choose drills that involve as many players and variety of skills as possible.

Here's another important point to keep in mind regarding the basics. Every sport has a unique language all its own, and to assume that every youngster on your team understands the lingo without an explanation is a big mistake. For example, if you're coaching a first-year peewee baseball team, don't expect the kid who is running toward second base to stop there when you yell at him to "hold up." He may not understand that you're telling him to stay at second and not to continue running toward third. Of course, once you've clearly explained this term, you can then use it with confidence. Remember, kids often take things literally. So always be very clear with your instructions and the terms you use—make sure every child understands what you mean. It'll make your practices more effective and enjoyable.

KNOW WHAT TO EXPECT FROM YOUR TEAM

Children are constantly changing both physically and emotionally. Coaches must be able to recognize the differences as well as the similarities in their players if the sports experience is going to be beneficial for everyone. To be unaware of or not concerned about individual differences generally results in a coach who favors players who are more mature and skilled at the expense of those who aren't.

Take the age, experience, and conditioning level of your athletes into consideration before placing any expectations on them. Remember, you can't possibly expect the players to learn everything that you know about the sport during the relatively short amount of time they'll be spending with you. Stay focused on the basics while building their skills.

All children are individuals with their own particular likes and dislikes, strengths and weaknesses. However, generally speaking, they possess certain characteristics that are dictated by their age. A good coach should be aware of these typical traits:

⊕ **Under age six.** If your team is made up of children in this age group, it is likely to be their first experience with a team sport. Your goal should be simply to introduce them to the sport's most basic elements. Keep it easy and fun; make sure they're having a good time.

⊕ **Ages six through eleven.** Most of the children who fall into this category begin developing interests in a wide range of activities. For many, playing sports is important, and they want to do it well. If you're coaching these kids, remember to focus on basic skill development. Help them build a good foundation.

⊕ **Ages twelve and thirteen.** Typically, kids this age already possess the basic skills needed to play the sport, but they want to improve them. As a good coach, it's your responsibility to coordinate practices that are stimulating and focused on sharpening the players' existing skills. Providing healthy competition is another way to encourage this growth. These kids are also at an age when the need for personal identity is heightened—more than ever before. If your team is made up of kids in this age group, try to get to know them on an individual level. (Of course, this is a great tip for building special coach-player bonds with kids of *all* ages.) Talk about things other than how to field a grounder. Ask how they're doing in school and what their favorite subjects are. Which TV shows do they enjoy? Who is their favorite athlete or which team do they root for? Most important, pay attention to their answers and use the information in your conversations during the course of the season. Let's say, for example, one of the kids told you of a certain pro hockey player he likes and you hear a story about that player. Be sure to mention it at the next game or practice. Bringing up such details shows that you listen to your players and care about them as people, not just as athletes.

⊕ **Age fourteen and older.** Teenagers are often the most difficult kids to coach. For many, it is a turbulent time during which they require authority but crave independence. Don't be surprised if you meet kids in this age group who possess know-it-all-attitudes and frown on any interaction with adults that involves constructive criticism, advice, or instruction. They are likely to be intent on showing you that they don't need your supervision or help in learning and developing skills. Furthermore, you may find that a number of these kids go to athletic camps and follow the sport you're coaching so closely that they may actually be more knowledgeable about it than you are in some aspects.

Don't let yourself feel threatened. Instead, embrace the opportunity as a way to enhance your coaching abilities. Children can be bright and resourceful—listen to them. Let them know that you value their opinions, suggestions, and other input regarding the team. By respecting them, you are likely to gain theirs. Keep the lines of communication open. For example, you might ask which drills they think are best to perform during practice. During games, ask their opinions on which approach they think might be best for certain situations. They will appreciate your interest, and it will help keep them focused and involved in the action.

Keep in mind that the characteristics provided in these categories are typical and have been presented to give you a *general* idea of what you might expect from your players. But above everything else—no matter what their age—always be supportive, sensitive, and encouraging. Maintaining such a positive attitude will help build the confidence and self-esteem of each individual on the team. It's a gift that will last.

BE FAIR TO ALL YOUR PLAYERS

More than 85 percent of today's volunteer coaches have their own sons or daughters on the team. Coaching your own child can be tricky at times, but if handled properly, it can be an extremely rewarding experience for both of you.

It's a natural tendency for some coaches to show preferential treatment toward their own children, perhaps by providing them with extra playing time, giving them more attention during practices, or putting them in charge of special tasks. On the other hand, some coaches have the opposite reaction toward their children and will go out of their way to avoid displaying preferential treatment. Showing favoritism will put your child in a tough position with the other kids on the team. And if you bench your child simply to avoid partiality, you'll appear to be favoring the other kids on the team over your own. Your child will be justifiably upset and conflict in your relationship is likely to occur. Ideally, your behavior should lie somewhere between these two extremes. Even without a child on the team, always strive to give equal time and attention to all of the players.

As for the special relationship you have with your own child, it is important that he or she understands and is made aware of your role as the coach. Consider the following suggestions:

☺ Explain to your child that being the coach is a great honor. Although he or she will be sort of "sharing" you with the other kids, it doesn't mean you love your child any less.

☺ With your child's help, put together a list of all the positives and negatives about being the coach. Resolve the negatives by working with your child to develop solutions. For instance, on the positive side, you might list that the two of you will be spending more time together than before, and that, as the coach, you'll ensure that your child and the rest of the team will have fun as they learn new skills. On the negative side, your child might expect to play a certain position simply because you are his or her parent. Explain that you must be fair to everyone and cannot show favoritism. Your child and his or her teammates will have an equal chance to play different positions.

☺ To effectively monitor how things are going, keep the communication lines open. It's important for your child to understand that he or she can come to you with a concern or problem at any time.

☺ Be sure to praise your child's willingness, understanding, and cooperation in this special venture.

Keep in mind that as the coach, it's your responsibility to help all of the players on your team. Taking the time to explain this to your child will help promote better understanding and avoid potential problems.

BE PREPARED TO DEAL WITH BAD BEHAVIOR

It's a simple but unfortunate fact of life that most people, even the most rational ones, behave irrationally at times. Be aware that such negative behavior is likely to occur, and it will come from parents and coaches, as well as the players themselves. As a good coach, you must be prepared to deal with these situations quickly and effectively. Problems that are ignored can undermine the attitude of the entire team and risk making the season miserable for everyone.

Although we're not citing parents specifically, they do, in fact, make up a significant number of the offenders and are often a coach's biggest headache. According to statistics compiled by the National Alliance For Youth Sports, 15 percent of parents are likely to act out of control at their child's athletic events, compared to just 5 percent five years ago. These figures are hardly surprising, considering this type of rage isn't limited to football fields and hockey rinks. It is taking place with alarming regularity on highways, in airports, at schools, and in the workplace, not to mention the disturbing increase of inappropriate, often violent behavior displayed among professional athletes. It seems that people everywhere are becoming increasingly impatient and short on understanding. They also tend to be vocal and quick to show their displeasure when things don't go their way.

In the world of youth sports, a combination of ego and intolerance for losing encourages this kind of negative behavior among players and spectators alike. Furthermore, many parents believe that future athletic scholarships, pro contracts, and endorsements for their children are at stake. On the positive side, the good news is that most parents are well behaved and offer positive support and encouragement. However, as a coach, you cannot close your eyes to the fact that an ever-increasing number of adults are losing control and venting their frustrations with rude and insensitive remarks; or, as we're seeing with the ugly rise in violent incidents across the youth sports landscape, with their fists.

During the season, you may find yourself playing against a team that's led by an out-of-control coach. He'll be pacing up and down the sidelines ranting and raving, belittling the kids who don't perform "well enough," and arguing every call that doesn't go his team's way. This type of coaching behavior is completely unacceptable. It has no place in youth sports.

In Chapter 5, we'll take a closer look at how to handle common problems that are likely to pop up during the course of a season among parents, opposing coaches, and even your own players. We'll also discuss ways to possibly prevent them from occurring at all.

SUMMING IT UP

Being a good volunteer coach takes a lot of time, effort, and dedication. Besides teaching skills to the youngsters on your team, you must be able to work well with parents, other coaches, and league administrators. After reading this chapter, you should have a basic idea of what's in store for you this season. Ready to go on? Let's start by focusing on those kids!

2. MEET THE KIDS

One of the truly fascinating aspects of coaching youth sports is that every child you'll come across will be remarkably different, and in so many ways. Even though many teams are comprised of players of similar ages, their athletic capabilities, personality traits, and emotional and physical developments are sure to span a broad spectrum. This is what makes coaching children so wonderfully challenging and rewarding, and let's not forget fun!

You're going to have a group of young athletes who are outgoing, dynamic, and strongly motivated to win; others will be more timid, less inspired, and not quite as passionate about the game. You'll be coaching kids who range from the athletically gifted and physically capable to those who are clumsy and lacking athletic skills. You're going to discover that what works when dealing with one child may backfire miserably with the next. Consequently, you will find yourself constantly challenged to find the right approach for successfully teaching, encouraging, and motivating each child.

Being aware of the many types of children you're likely to encounter during your coaching experience is a big step toward understanding how to relate to them. Ready for an overview? Okay, let's meet the kids.

THE GIFTED ATHLETE

For some reason, there always seems to be at least one child on just about every youth sports team whose athletic ability stands out from all the others. Whether it's their speed, strength, size, coordination, or a combination of all of the above, these kids will carry around the unofficial label of "team stars." Performing like miniature Michael Jordans or Mia Hamms, these players are certainly fun to watch, and just as much fun to coach. Furthermore, they make your job easier because, typically, they require less one-on-one instruction time.

Quite often, these kids have simply been blessed with a natural athletic ability. Their skill levels are significantly superior to their teammates, especially during the earlier years when many children have not yet started to develop hand-eye coordination and other basic motor skills. Gifted athletes, whose superior ability will be quite noticeable to you after only a practice or two, can play a very important role on your team. Provided that they have good attitudes—not arrogant, condescending, or critical of the other players—they can emerge as team leaders and wonderful role models. It's up to you to guide them into such a positive position. For instance, when giving instructions on how to throw a pass, lay down a bunt, or properly throw in a soccer ball from the sidelines, these gifted players can assist you in demonstrating the right techniques. And if they typically exhibit positive attitudes and sound practice habits, you can point out these attributes—without showing favoritism, of course—as the model for the other kids on the team to emulate.

One of the greatest tasks of coaching "superstars" is making sure that they grow and are constantly improving their skills. This means keeping them challenged. In many cases, youngsters who start off the season with obvious talent are likely to receive less attention from the coach during practice sessions. After all, it's only natural for coaches to gravitate toward the child who is having trouble fielding grounders rather than work with the one who consistently fields them cleanly. However, a good coach realizes the importance of challenging these talented players during practice. For instance, when hitting grounders during baseball practice, make sure to "mix it up" when hitting balls to the talented players— hit some with a little more speed or a little further out of range than normal. Or make the child backhand the balls or dive to catch them. Subtle moves such as these will keep the more talented athletes from becoming stagnant or bored while enhancing their skills.

Also, be careful of the tendency to pile too much praise on your gifted athletes. This is easy to do as they continually scoop up grounders cleanly or rarely miss a lay-up. Although praise and support are certainly important, just don't go overboard with it—and the reasons should be obvious. First, too many accolades may cause these children to feel unnecessary pressure, which can impede their positive attitude and performance. Having to earn your constant praise can take all the fun out of playing. After all, when these kids strike out or miss scoring the winning goal, they may feel personally responsible for the loss. In an effort to diminish your high expectations, they may subconsciously hold back from playing to the best of their ability or further developing their skills.

Another problem you'll risk by overloading praise on certain kids is resentment from the other players. Construing this as favoritism, the "overlooked" members of the team may harbor negative feelings toward both you and the children you tend to fuss over.

Once again, as a coach, there's certainly nothing wrong with enjoying the talents of the gifted children on your team. Just remember to keep them challenged and motivated without showing favoritism. Maintain a proper perspective—you have an *entire team* that needs your guidance and support.

THE NON-ATHLETIC CHILD

Let's face it, you're going to have kids on your team who aren't as skilled or coordinated as a lot of their teammates. Ground balls consistently "pass through" their gloves; footballs never seem to stay in their grip; and dribbled basketballs are generally bounced off their feet. The fact is that some kids are not athletically inclined, and it's these youngsters who are going to require extra time, attention, and words of encouragement. They are also the ones who are most likely to test your patience and understanding.

When it comes to non-athletic children, it's important to remember that they are doing the best they can. These are the kids who are constantly battling overwhelming feelings of frustration and inadequacy for not being able to perform at the levels of many of their friends and teammates. When they can't seem to execute a skill accurately, even though you have demonstrated it repeatedly during practice, carefully choose your words when providing further instruction. Don't ever bury them in feelings of guilt or shame for their athletic inabilities. And be sure to avoid sending any negative signals through your body language.

Always try to balance any constructive criticism with a few words of encouragement. If possible, mention something positive that you noticed when they were up at bat or in the field or on the court. Of course, this is a good practice when dealing with all of the players on your team, not just the ones who are lacking skills. A good coach, however, will understand that these children may need an extra helping of support. Try to make a conscious effort to be on alert for any improvements these kids display, and then be sure to use them as confidence boosters.

It's your responsibility to recognize and value each child's contribution to the team, no matter how big or how small it may be. Instill in each child a genuine sense of belonging. At times, this can be extremely tough, but realize that every one of those kids offers something. Okay, so they may not make the game-winning plays, but, even better, they may display a never-give-up attitude, a good sense of humor, or simply a sincere effort. It doesn't really matter what it is, as long as each child feels valued by the coach and his or her teammates. When your players are out there doing their best, it's important that they all know how much you appreciate their effort and commitment. Every practice and each game provides you with an opportunity to convey your feelings to them.

If the child is grossly mismatched with the sport and the parents ask your advice on whether or not their child should continue playing, be honest and helpful. Explain that in spite of the child's limitation in this one particular area, other sports may be more suitable in complementing his or her abilities. Suggest specific sports that, potentially, may provide their child with the opportunity to achieve a successful athletic experience.

THE SHY ATHLETE

Shyness is one of the more common social problems found in

Beware
the Short Attention Span

Virtually all children have short attention spans. Typically, the younger the child, the shorter the attention span, and the more difficult it will be for you to hold their focus. It's a simple fact—if the kids aren't interested in what you're saying or doing, their minds are going to stray.

There are lots of distractions at youth athletic events that can easily disrupt a child's focus on the task at hand and make your job that much trickier. For instance, if you're coaching an outdoor sport, youngsters may be more interested in the colorful butterfly floating around than the baseball that's heading right toward them. Young outfielders may busy themselves picking dandelions or swatting at bees. And don't be surprised if the players on both teams turn their heads in unison at the sound of an ice cream truck making its way down the street. Distractions abound at indoor games as well, where children may be more interested in waving to Grandma in the third row or posing for Dad's video camera than guarding the player with the ball.

The quickest and easiest way to eliminate the problem of short attention spans at practice is to incorporate lots of activity into the sessions. When players are on the move, they're more apt to be having fun, and the physical activity encourages learning and skill development. When players are sitting or standing still, fun comes to a screeching halt. If practices are fun, even the uninterested players will be more likely to stay focused and become active participants.

So don't overwhelm your players with long lectures and endless instructions. If you bog them down with too much information, they will quickly tune you out. Keep your instructions clear and concise, don't speak in generalities or use unfamiliar terms, get to the point, use inflection, be animated, and speak with enthusiasm. When choosing physical activities, stay away from long, boring laps and tedious drills. Don't make the kids endure endless lines while waiting for their turns to kick the ball or swing the bat. Basically, you've got to create a practice environment that minimizes listening time and maximizes effective participation. You must be as helpful, understanding, and as patient as you are when teaching your own children something new.

Finally, keep in mind that a child's lack of focus may be attributed to attention deficit hyperactivity disorder (ADHD), which usually appears before the age of seven. According to the National Attention Deficit Disorder Association, the most common characteristics of a child with ADHD are distractibility (poor sustained attention to tasks), impulsivity (impaired impulse control and delay of gratification), and hyperactivity (excessive activity and physical restlessness). If you think someone on your team may be showing signs of ADHD, talk to his or her parents about your concerns.

childhood. While there are varying degrees of shyness, the most common characteristic of shy children is their ability to blend in with a group. This is something that you should be keenly aware of because shy athletes are easily overlooked by coaches. Typically, they're not vocal, they follow instructions, they don't ask for help, and they don't disrupt practice as they quietly flow from drill to drill.

If you have shy children on your team, your abilities will be tested as you try to gently coax them out of their self-imposed isolation and get them involved and interacting with the group. It's not as easy as it may sound. If you push too hard, these children may become frightened or overwhelmed and pull back even further into their protective shells. Some may simply quit the team and give up on sports entirely.

Because shy children devote lots of energy dodging attention and blending into the background, the last thing they want is to be put into a situation in which all eyes are focused on them. Being singled out by the coach is a prime example, so it's up to you to come up with non-threatening ways to help them overcome their shyness and feel comfortable with both you and the team. For instance, at the start of one of your practice sessions, consider selecting a shy child along with two or three others to lead the warm-up drill. This is a small but effective step in helping that child get comfortable in front of the group without making him or her feel isolated. Coming up with ways to slowly ease anxiety is the key to helping children conquer shyness. And remember to be gradual. Pushing these kids too hard or too quickly can be traumatic, causing them to feel more fear and discomfort than they already do.

Shy children live in a scary and intimidating world in which they feel isolated and lonely. If their shyness is not addressed during the formative years, it can have long-term negative effects. Don't allow them to hang back in the shadows. Doing so will only reinforce their behavior as an acceptable way to negotiate through life.

As a coach, you are in the position to make a positive difference in the lives of the shy children on your team. Lend them a hand in developing a solid foundation of athletic and social skills, and they'll discover that being part of the team is a fun-filled experience. Encouraging them to venture out of their private existence will help them discover an inner courage they never realized they had.

THE DISCIPLINE PROBLEM

Children are going to test the boundaries of what you consider acceptable and unacceptable behavior—and some will test those limits more than others. And you're going to have to be ready to handle it. Whether you like it or not, children who misbehave at home or school are probably going to bring the same unwelcomed traits to their practices and games. Discipline problems can range from talking back and picking on teammates to ignoring instructions and getting involved in physical fights with the other players.

At the beginning of the season, it is critical to lay down the ground rules. Let your team know exactly what you consider unacceptable behavior. Be very clear about it. If you don't assert yourself from the start, you'll lose control of the team, and quickly! If kids sense that you don't mean business, it will open the door to all sorts of trouble that can linger throughout the season. When one of your players has ventured into unacceptable territory, be sure to address it, and make the child accountable for his or her actions in some way. Depending on the infraction, this could mean benching the kid for a few minutes or for the remainder of the game. Make it clear to the child and to the rest of the team that you are in a position of authority and will not tolerate any unacceptable behavior. Consequences will be enforced, and enforced consistently, without exception.

Some coaches who are overly concerned with winning are often guilty of stretching their disciplinary rules to accommodate infractions from the more gifted players. Don't do it! Compromising team rules can place a serious strain on the dynamics of the entire team. If you allow a player to get away with unacceptable behavior, you are sending the message that he or she is more important than the others. It will plant seeds of resentment, conflict, and dissension within the team. Furthermore, shifting the balance of power to the player you have let off the hook will undermine your own authority. Finally, and perhaps most serious, you will lose respect in the eyes of everyone, including the kid you didn't hold accountable.

Again, lay down the ground rules early in the season, and when a rule is broken, don't turn a blind eye to it. Address the infraction and hold the player accountable. Specific discipline tactics are discussed in Chapter 5.

YOUNGSTERS WITH SPECIAL NEEDS

As a volunteer coach, you may question your own qualifications, talents, and abilities to work with children who have special needs. These kids can include those with disabilities ranging from hearing loss and vision impairment to medical conditions such as asthma, epilepsy, and diabetes. Children with Down syndrome and those who do not have full use of their limbs also fall into this category. But good coaches will understand that every child on the team is different; they already appreciate the unique qualities of each.

Not only will children with special needs reap obvious benefits by being included on a team, their teammates will benefit from their participation as well. Players will be encouraged to develop patience, tolerance, and understanding as they recognize the differences among themselves and their teammates.

In order for most children with special needs to participate, certain accommodations are necessary. Such rule modifications are not designed to give the child or the team an unfair advantage; they are simply made to help remove some of the child's barriers. Of course, these accommodations will vary, depending on the child's particular needs. For instance, a child with Down syndrome who is part of a baseball team may be allowed an extra swing or two when up at bat. The child with limited use of his legs, but who wants to be part of a basketball team to be with his friends, shouldn't be stuck on the sidelines in a wheelchair and given the job of team scorekeeper. As the coach, you can help this child become more of a contributing player. Perhaps you can appoint him as the designated free-thrower for the team, and let him take the free throws (or every other one). Accommodations such as these will give the youngsters with special needs specific and important roles on the team without disrupting the participation of the other players. And at practices, just like all the other children, they will have specific skills to work on and try to improve.

Remember, kids with disabilities are children first and foremost. Those who wish to be part of a youth sports team deserve that opportunity. Their participation, which is their legal right, can be done safely and without major disruption to the team or league. Regardless of their physical limitations or abilities, all

Offer Equal Opportunity

Coaches are often guilty of stereotyping kids without even realizing it. A baseball coach, for instance, may assume that a physically stocky kid will make a good catcher and stick him behind home plate for the entire season. The athletically gifted child may be sent to the pitcher's mound. Meanwhile, that "catcher" may be more interested in and suited for playing first base, while that "pitcher" may be a more effective outfielder. But you'll never uncover your players' hidden talents and skills—and neither will they—if you don't give them the chance. Forcing them into one role, especially at an early age, infringes on their growth, limits learning, and risks spoiling the entire sports experience.

Particularly at the younger age levels, be sure to talk to the kids and find out which positions interest them the most, and then take it from there. You're probably going to have to do some juggling, especially if every child wants to be the pitcher or the goalie or the forward. But through the course of a season, during games and practices, you'll be able to rotate the positions so that each child gets to experience as many facets of the game as possible.

You may find it in everyone's best interest to put the more skilled players at certain positions, especially early in the season. For instance, a child who is struggling to catch the ball shouldn't be playing first base for a couple reasons. First, there is a higher risk of injury, as a substantial number of balls are likely to be thrown to the first baseman; and second, the child may find it embarrassing to continually miss catching the ball. As a good coach, your job would be to help this child develop catching skills before trying him or her out at first base.

It's a good idea to devise a rotation schedule to ensure equal playing time for your players. The dreaded bench is pretty uncomfortable, especially to a child's self-esteem. Youngsters who sit on the bench are not going to be learning or having any fun. Studies have confirmed that the overwhelming majority of children would rather play for a losing team than sit on the bench for a winning one.

In the interest of fair play and good sportsmanship, always think of yourself as an "equal opportunity" leader. Your efforts will be appreciated.

kids should have the chance to participate, learn, and be challenged. As the coach, you can help make this happen.

THE AVERAGE KID

Sure you're going to have the occasional child who will be disruptive and challenge your authority. And yes, you may have to exhibit lots of patience to help lure a shy child from a protective shell. You may even be lucky enough to work with an exceptionally gifted young athlete. But for the most part, you're going to be involved with a regular group of kids with average skills who simply want to have some fun with their friends and play a sport they've either enjoyed in the past or may be trying for the first time.

Most children enjoy being part of a group, and what their

friends are involved in usually plays a big role in what they are willing to try. If their best friends are signing up for hockey or baseball, they'll probably want to sign up as well. If they see a sport on TV that sparks their interest, they may want to give it a shot.

Usually anywhere from age ten through twelve, some of these "average" children will decide—often subconsciously— that they have a genuine interest in being part of a youth sports team and want to continue the activity. A lot of these kids discover they love the competition; others want to become better skilled; some just enjoy the social interaction; still others are excited simply to be part of a team.

No matter what the reason, these kids will begin to develop a deep-rooted love of the sport, and their behavior and attitude toward playing on a team will become more serious and mature as they continue to grow. They'll embrace the dedication and training, as well as the commitments and sacrifices that must be made in order to become the best that they can be. And you will be there to help encourage and nurture this precious, positive attitude.

SUMMING IT UP

All of the children who make up your team will be different. They will have various backgrounds, personalities, and skills, but *all* will require your attention, care, and concern. As a good coach, it is important to make sure that each and every child feels special, that they have a fun and rewarding experience. As you develop your team over the course of the season, remember the various approaches you can take with the different personality types. Use them to enhance their experience, as well as your own.

3. Meet the Parents

Although there's a lot of parent bashing taking place these days, the simple fact is that the majority of youth sports parents are a supportive and caring group, and they do a wonderful job with their children. Parenting isn't easy. In fact, it has become increasingly difficult in a society where being average just doesn't seem to be good enough anymore, especially when it comes to raising children. But without parental involvement, organized sports would quickly fade away. The problem is that an increasing number of parents—although in the minority—are disrupting youth sports programs with their unrealistic expectations, fiery tempers, and out-of-control behavior.

Human behavior is complex, and when it comes to organized sports, this subject can be even trickier to understand. Why some parents behave badly when watching their children's athletic performances is usually due to factors that are out of your control. Perhaps a particular parent recently lost his or her job, is going through a painful divorce, or is dealing with a serious health matter. Whatever the circumstances, one thing is certain—parents and their highly combustible mixture of personalities will show up at the field or the court or the ball park, armed with their own set of expectations, wants, and needs. How successful you are in relating to each parent will have a significant impact on everyone's level of enjoyment during the season.

This chapter will provide you with an overview of the types of moms and dads you're likely to encounter. Ready? Time to meet the parents.

THE GOLDEN PARENT

A lot of truly great parents fall into this category, and deservedly so. These are the ones who genuinely care about the sports experience for everyone involved, and will do just about anything to ensure a smooth-running season for their children, the team, and the coach.

Golden parents enjoy the hoopla and excitement of the games, but they don't go overboard. Always maintaining the spirit of fun and enjoyment, they heartily cheer for every child on the team, offering encouragement and support whenever appropriate. They are also models of good sportsmanship by applauding good plays made by the opposition, and congratulating everyone—winners and losers—on a game well played. Understanding that playing sports is only one facet of a child's growth and development, golden parents maintain a healthy perspective, knowing that over-emphasizing performance and winning will detract from the enjoyment of the activity. These parents keep their negative emotions in check, recognizing that they are role models and their behavior will make a lasting impression on *every* child who is playing on the field, as well as those who are watching from the stands.

Appreciative and respectful of your role as coach, these parents are the ones who eagerly step forward at a moment's notice to lend a hand whenever needed. They recognize the scope of your responsibilities, and often get involved with tasks such as arranging car pools, taking charge of team fund raisers, and helping out at practices and during games. They are usually the first ones to help chaperone post-game trips for ice cream or pizza, and make sure that there is always water available for thirsty players during games.

If you've got parents like these who are willing to help ease the responsibilities of the coaching job, encourage them. And be sure to recognize them at your season-ending banquet or team get-together. While most of these parents don't perform the duties for attention, they certainly deserve acknowledgment as a sign of your gratitude.

THE OVER-INVOLVED PARENT

At some point, every parent with a child who is involved in organized sports will confront the question of where encouragement stops and pushing begins. When it comes to their children and sports, this dilemma has perplexed adults for years.

It's certainly no secret that parents want their children to succeed in every activity they're involved in. It doesn't matter if it's a spelling bee, a piano recital, a school play, or a baseball game. It's just that when it comes to sports, lots of parents find their level of interest reaching newfound heights. For many, the underlying reason for this strong interest is that they themselves haven't been able to make an impression in the sports world—never scored the game-winning touchdown, home run, or goal during their own sports experience—and are trying to achieve that mark through their children. They could also be the ones who struck out in the last inning or missed scoring the game-winning goal during a youth-league championship game twenty-five years ago, and they want to make sure their own children don't suffer the same fate. Perhaps the most intense over-involved parent is the one who was once a star athlete and has the same expectations for his or her child.

Over-involved parents typically struggle—and generally fail—to detach their own self-images from their children's. When their kids make mistakes during a game or basically don't live up to athletic expectations, these parents view such "failures" as their own, not the child's.

Aside from tarnishing the relationship with their children, over-involved parents can be a real burden for the entire team. They are often the know-it-alls who believe their ideas regarding how a coach should manage the team are the best. Through loud and obvious criticism, they undermine the coach's authority. All it takes is the presence of one of these zealous individuals to quickly drain the fun from the program and turn everyone's participation into a miserable ordeal. Furthermore, parents who make spectacles of themselves in this way are an embarrassment to their children, who have to endure their outbursts. The unacceptable behavior of the over-involved parent interferes with healthy competition in what should be a fun, low-pressure environment.

THE WIN-AT-ALL-COSTS PARENT

In today's world of youth athletics, which is sadly becoming increasingly competitive, too many parents view the games as battles between two enemies. These parents, who are obsessed with winning games and championships, plague sports programs throughout the country. Blinded by their visions of first-place trophies and post-season glory, these types often resort to any means possible to ensure a win for their child's team. If it means intimidating an official into making more calls in their team's favor, they'll do it. If it means convincing the coach to play only the most athletic kids and benching the rest, they'll do it. If it means pushing their injured children back into the game before they're physically ready, they'll even do that.

To the win-at-all-costs parent, winning games is equated with success, regardless of how it's achieved. And losing translates into catastrophic failure—something that is considered unacceptable. Such unhealthy emphasis on a game's outcome, rather than focus on the effort, participation, and growth of the players (both as individuals and as a team), places unnecessary pressure on the entire group.

When these parents show up at the end of a game, the first words out of their mouths are usually, "Did you win?" or "How much did you win by?" After all, to them, what the scoreboard says at the end of the game is all that matters— much more important than whether the children had fun or made any progress with the skills of the sport. With such a warped focus on the end result, these parents are teaching their kids that the outcome of a game is more important than fun and learning.

PROFESSIONAL-LEAGUE PARENT

Plenty of parents these days invest lots of time, money, and energy into their children's sports experiences—and they want their money's worth. Some become overly enthusiastic, savoring as much success and entertainment as they can from the experience. These are the parents who watch from the stands or the sidelines and see miniature professionals out there on the field—not children who are merely participating in a game. For them, the ten-year-old child playing youth league baseball or softball, for example, is a smaller version of a major leaguer.

Youth sports can provide a golden opportunity for parents to become immersed in their children's team if they want to. Throughout the course of a season, many parents who regularly attend the games strike up friendships with the other parents and get to know all of the kids on the team very well. This type of bonding fuels growing interest in the team, and encourages some parents to become die-hard fans with an intense desire to see the kids perform well. Games suddenly take on a whole new meaning for these parents, and they root for the team with the same intensity—and the same expectations—as they have for a professional one.

Of course, it's a wonderful thing when parents root for their children and cheer on the team. Camaraderie among parents is positive, as well. The problem occurs when this support reaches over-the-top levels and becomes too intense. Suddenly, these professional-league parents begin applying unrealistically high standards to a group of kids who are clearly not pros. They become riveted to the action, as every play becomes immensely important. Each game the team wins is monumental, and every loss a heartbreaker. As the parents focus almost exclusively on winning, they begin to compromise all the positive values that they might have fostered at one time.

THE IMMATURE PARENT

The childish behavior seen in youth sports today often doesn't take place on the playing field—it's on the sidelines and in the stands.

Although most parents do not intentionally set out to exhibit immature behavior, they sometimes get caught up in the excitement surrounding the game. Immature parents tend to act out impulsively, often without considering the consequences. They are quick to make derogatory remarks at the official who makes a call against their team ("Forget your glasses, Ump? Too bad. You're missing a great game."); or they place the blame for a botched play on the coach ("Why did you put in a sub *now*, Coach? You know that kid can't run!). They also applaud when an opposing player is involved in a bad play, and boo when he or she does well. They are true models of unsportsmanlike conduct.

Because of their immaturity, some of these parents aren't aware of the enormous impact of their poor behavior. Others simply don't care. Children take their cues from parents and other adults. When they see a parent applaud a child on the opposing team who makes a bad play, make fun of an official, or insult their coach, you can be sure they will perceive this kind of behavior as acceptable—a kind of permission slip to behave in the same manner. Bad behavior breeds bad behavior; it's a vicious and destructive cycle.

THE STATUS-CONSCIOUS PARENT

There's simply no denying that parents become filled with pride as they watch their children sink baskets, score touchdowns, and hit home runs. After all, when their kids perform like champions, they feel like champions, too. It's only natural to feel this sense of pride, but when the desire becomes too powerful, it can cause tunnel vision in the way they perceive their children.

Status-conscious "sports" parents are those who are most

thrilled if their children are successful athletes—more than being successful in any other area. In their minds, and in the minds of their friends, neighbors, and relatives (or so they think), it means that they are good parents. Some of these parents don't show the same degree of enthusiasm toward their children whose talents lie in non-athletic areas. They would much rather their kids to be throwing spirals than playing the flute.

MONEY-DRIVEN PARENT

There's a lot of money to be made in sports these days, and parents are well aware of the cash windfalls that an athletically gifted child can generate. But when visions of athletic stardom—with its college scholarships, multi-million dollar professional contracts, hefty signing bonuses, and product endorsements—become the focal point of parental thinking, the results are typically disastrous.

Money-driven parents are guilty of thinking too far ahead. They worry that their children won't be chosen for the all-star team, or won't be good enough to make the travel team or the high school varsity (in the next six or seven years or so). They are obsessed with the athletic futures of their offspring—and often delusional about their abilities. If you have to deal with this type of parent, anticipate some pressure. They will expect you to give their children maximum playing time, and if you don't, they will blame you for robbing their children of a future scholarship or a position on a professional team.

In order to gain an edge, these parents have even been known to hold their children back a grade in school. This way, the kids will be older, more mature, and hopefully more talented than the rest of the pool of players—anything to make their children stand out. These parents see their youngsters as personal lottery tickets to fame and fortune. Despite the staggering odds against it, they firmly believe that if they push their children hard enough and long enough, they'll reach the sacred ground of the professional ranks.

A MATTER OF ABUSE

Most of the parental types presented in this chapter can be considered mentally or emotionally abusive—at least to some degree. Those who place unrealistic expectations on their children, wanting them to win every game, score the most points, and play without error, are guilty. Although emotional abuse is often more subtle than the physical type, it can be equally devastating. Youngsters who endure unnecessary pressure from parents, especially during critical periods of growth and development, are likely to be haunted by the resulting scars for a lifetime. Whether on the playing field, in the classroom, or at home, most children who are constantly expected to excel will eventually meet with failure. And these expectations can dominate their existence, draining spirit and self-esteem.

As a quality coach, you can help counteract such emotional abuse by maintaining a positive atmosphere during games and practices. Show unwavering support to your players. Build their confidence and strengthen their self-esteem.

SUMMING IT UP

So there you have them—the typical parents you may (or may not) encounter during your coaching experience. Keep in mind that these are the "classics," and there are many more types you are likely to meet. As a good coach, if you have a basic understanding of the kinds of parents you'll be seeing during the course of the season, you'll be better prepared to deal with them and diffuse any potential problems. You'll also have greater insight into why some children behave the way they do. After all, if mom and dad act a certain way, Johnny or Mary may exhibit some of the same characteristics.

Keep in mind that most parents are great—those exhibiting problematic behavior are in the minority. And don't make the mistake of judging parents during your initial meeting; they may very well surprise you. The ones you may perceive as "nutty" or "strict" or "intense" could turn out to be model parents once the season begins. Furthermore, for some parents, this may be their first experience having a child in youth sports. To a degree, it will be up to you to guide them—to set the tone as to what you expect from them and their children. Chapter 4 presents some guidelines to help you achieve this.

4. Be Prepared

Coaching youth sports, although a rewarding undertaking, can be pretty challenging as well. The better prepared you are for the various obstacles that are likely to arise during the course of a season, the less likely you'll be to stumble over them. Think of it this way, in order to do well on a test, you have to prepare by studying the material. To increase your chances of being a hit in a job interview, it's best to prepare a resumé and do some research on the prospective employer. It's no different in the world of coaching youth sports. Preparation is imperative for building a solid foundation for a successful season.

Just because you will be coaching a sport that you once played yourself, don't think you're automatically prepared for the position. Coaches who think they can just show up for practices without a plan and expect that everything will fall magically into place during games are in for a rather unpleasant surprise. It just doesn't work that way. Poor preparation and lack of planning will quickly drag you down a disastrous and miserable path. And you'll be taking the kids and their parents along with you.

Before the start of the season, most youth sports programs sponsor basic training clinics for their volunteer coaches. The purpose of these clinics is to inform the coaches of the job responsibilities that lie ahead. Some programs are very basic while others, such as the National Youth Sports Coaches Association coaching clinics (see page 39), are much more comprehensive. All are designed to set you on the right course in becoming a top-quality coach. This chapter supports these efforts, and illustrates how preparedness is a major key. As the first order of business, you'll learn the importance of developing a sound coaching philosophy. You'll then see how holding a well-planned preseason parents meeting is a vital step in getting off to a good start. Finally, you'll receive guidelines on basic pregame preparations, as well as safety guidelines.

DEVELOP A COACHING PHILOSOPHY

When you get right down to it, developing a coaching philosophy—a mission statement that reflects the goals you hope to achieve and the standards you expect to maintain with your team—is pretty easy. It's living up to it during every practice and at each game that's the real challenge. Your coaching philosophy is likely to evolve, at least in part, from within you— the manner in which you conduct yourself and deal with people on a daily basis. It's an expression of your own personality, values, and beliefs.

As discussed in Chapter 1, as a good coach, your philosophy should reflect a number of considerations—all focusing on the best interest of your players. First and foremost, it should take into account the well-being of *every* child on the team, not just those who run faster, throw harder, or catch better. A sound philosophy encourages players to exhibit patience and understanding. It promotes respect of self, as well as that of teammates, coaches, officials, and players on opposing teams. Ethics, fair play, good sportsmanship, honesty, integrity, and team spirit are standard. A good philosophy must stress fun over winning and the progress of each child over the development of all-stars. It's about doing things for the benefit of all youngsters.

As a good volunteer coach, be sure to have a firm grasp on your philosophy. It should be a clear vision that you are able to translate to your players and their parents. Don't rely on the philosophy of others—your favorite high school soccer or football coach. Find your own niche. Above all else, think

National Youth Sports Coaches Association (NYSCA)

 The National Youth Sports Coaches Association provides training, support, and continuing education to its members who volunteer to coach youth sports teams. Training sessions cover topics such as coaching philosophies, tips for effective practice sessions, game fundamentals, injury prevention and treatment, and the importance of role modeling. Since the early 1980s, the NYSCA, which now has over 2,500 chapters nationwide, has helped volunteers understand the psychology of coaching children, and has shown them how to enhance their relationship with parents, officials, and kids. For more information, contact the NYSCA at 1-800-688-KIDS or visit its website at www.nays.org.

about the children; look into your heart and lead them in the direction you know is right.

It won't take long for you to discover if your coaching philosophy is a winner, if it needs some minor revisions, or if it should be tossed into the trash. Smiles etched on the faces of your team at practices and games, or comments from the kids indicating that they hope to play for you next year are clear signs that your philosophy is a good one. On the other hand, if parents aren't thanking you for how much fun their children are having, if the kids are regularly skipping practices and games, and if no one is clamoring to be on your team next season, chances are your methods need some alterations.

Your philosophy says a great deal about who you are both as a coach and as a person. So put some serious thought into it, and always keep the well-being of each child your main concern. It'll be worth the effort.

HOLD A PRESEASON PARENTS MEETING

How well you communicate with the parents or guardians of your young athletes will have a huge impact on the level of everyone's enjoyment during the season. One of the most important things you can do before stepping onto the field with your team is to conduct a preseason meeting with these people.

This meeting will serve several key purposes. First, it will give you an opportunity to introduce yourself to the parents of your players within a casual atmosphere. It will also allow the parents to meet each other, encouraging camaraderie and friendliness. A preseason meeting will provide a forum for you to outline your coaching philosophy and discuss your goals and expectations for the upcoming season.

This meeting is the perfect place to distribute any consent

and/or medical forms that are required by most leagues, and learn of any players who may require special considerations. It's also a place for you to verbally acknowledge the important role of these parents in youth sports, and encourage them to show further support by volunteering their time in various ways throughout the season. Perhaps most important, holding this meeting demonstrates to the parents that you care enough about their children to take the time to meet with everyone *before* the season gets underway.

How you interact with the parents of your players will play a major role in setting the tone for the future. The first impression you make will be a lasting one, so approach this meeting with the same diligence and care that you would if you were meeting with an important client. If you are uncomfortable speaking in front of people, being prepared can be the best antidote. Jot down all of the points you want to cover on a notepad, then hold onto it throughout the meeting and refer to it as needed. Prior to the meeting, practice what you're going to say in front of a mirror or in front of a friend or family member. Keep in mind that no one expects you to be a great orator, a stand-up comic, or a motivational speaker. Most parents will already have a built in respect for you and will support you and your agenda.

The more comfortable the parents feel with you, the better your chances will be of having an open and constructive relationship with them. So make an effort to talk to each parent individually at this orientation meeting, and acknowledge them when they show up at practices and games.

Sample Agenda

There are many ways in which you can conduct your meeting.

Programs such as the Parents Association for Youth Sports (PAYS), presented in the inset below, can help. The following sample agenda offers some general guidelines for your consideration. Depending on the league, the particular sport, and your personal needs, these guidelines may vary.

BEGIN WITH AN INTRODUCTION

Start the meeting by introducing yourself to the group and welcoming them to the team. If you have a child on the team, chances are you'll already know some of the parents through

Parents Association for Youth Sports (PAYS)

The PAYS membership program, sponsored by the National Alliance For Youth Sports, is designed to help coaches outline important topics for parents regarding their children and youth sports. Ideally presented during a preseason meeting with parents, this program, which takes about thirty minutes, includes a short video and addresses issues such as good sportsmanship, the ramifications of negative behavior displayed by parents and other spectators, the importance of supporting a child's sports performance, and the consequences of pressuring a child with unrealistic expectations. Parents who go through the program also sign a Parents Code of Ethics, pledging to adhere to a standard of good behavior. For additional information, call 1-800-688-KIDS and ask to speak with a PAYS staff member or visit its website at www.nays.org.

school or community activities. To further break the ice, you might also consider having those in attendance introduce themselves. This is a good time to present your coaching philosophy and goals for the upcoming season. Also explain your personal ground rules, including the type of behavior you expect from the players, as well as the conduct you consider acceptable (and unacceptable) from the parents as well.

Be sure to stress the fact that the best interest of their children is always your number-one priority. Your goal is to help them develop certain basic skills that are essential to the sport, and grow within a healthy competitive environment. But above all, you want them to have fun.

SPELL OUT THE BASICS

In order to maintain a season that runs smoothly, it's important to present some basic team information to the parents. Start by handing out a schedule that includes dates, times, and locations of the games. Provide information on the days and times for practices, making sure to cite where they will be held and how long they will last. Also state the policy for rainy days if you're coaching an outdoor sport.

Along with the game schedule, it is also recommended that you pass out copies of a team roster that includes the names, addresses, and phone contacts of all of the players on your team, as well as your own. Throughout the season, parents will find it helpful having this contact information in one convenient location, especially when arranging car pools and organizing rainy-day phone chains. Making your own phone number available also shows that you are open to speaking with them at any time—to answer their questions or discuss any concerns.

Make the parents aware of any equipment or items the kids should bring to practices and games, including water bottles, bats, balls, and any protective equipment. While you are on this subject, be sure to tell the parents about the equipment that is provided by the league, as well as those items for which they are personally responsible. Many leagues provide uniforms, but the players are responsible for keeping them clean and in good repair before turning them back in at the end of the season. Inform parents of any safety equipment that is either recommended or required by the league. If players are responsible for items such as mouth guards, chest protectors, and shin guards, you might suggest places to make these purchases.

If there is a tournament in which you'd like to have your team participate, bring it up at this time. Also explain that tournaments and other special events require entry fees. See how the parents feel about participating. Fundraisers, which can range from selling candy and bumper stickers to sponsoring car washes and "team" garage sales, are a great way to generate money—and the kids can participate as well. They also help promote team spirit as the group works together toward a common goal.

Be sure to cover any program rules or policies of which they should be aware. For example, if you're coaching a baseball team, the league may limit the number of innings a child is allowed to pitch each week. Or the football program you're involved with may allow only certain types of cleats to be worn. Present any other specific modifications of the sport as dictated by the league rulebook. Finally, discuss the league's behavioral expectations of spectators and players, as well as any disciplinary procedures it may enforce.

DISTRIBUTE FORMS

Virtually all leagues require a number of standard forms—parental/guardian consent, medical evaluation, and emergency-treatment authorization—for each player. These forms, which your league will provide, must be properly filled out and returned to the league administration before the child can participate. Your preseason parents meeting is the perfect forum for distributing and explaining these forms.

Although each of the forms may vary somewhat in content and style, their intentions are basically the same. The *parental/guardian consent form* states that when a child plays a sport of any kind, there is an inherent possibility of getting injured. And in the event of an injury, the league is not responsible. (Most programs carry insurance against possible litigation. As a coach, be sure you ask about the league's coverage and your own status under the policy.)

The *medical evaluation form,* which is to be signed by the child's physician, basically states the child is physically able to participate in the sport. If the child has a certain condition, it is entered on this sheet. Some forms require immunization records as well.

The *emergency-treatment authorization form* is signed by the child's parent or guardian. Typically, it lists the names of one or two people to contact in the event the child is injured and requires emergency medical treatment. If these contacts can't be reached, this form gives the coach/league the authority to seek medical treatment for the child.

These and any other required forms should be explained to you in detail during the league's orientation meeting for coaches.

ENCOURAGE PARENTAL INVOLVEMENT

Most parents invest a lot of time, money, and energy into their children's sports activities. And you'll find that many are willing to volunteer their efforts during the season to help you out, as well as insure a positive experience for their kids. They are usually more than willing to pitch in to help make things run smoothly.

Occasionally, you may come across parents who will do everything in their power to avoid getting involved. They are the ones who are likely to appear at practices and games only long enough to drop their children off and pick them up. These parents, who are guilty of using the program as a baby-sitting service for a few hours every week, are not the norm. You'll find that the overwhelming majority will take an active interest in their children, and will be eager to help out.

There are a number of ways in which parents may be able to lend a hand. For instance, throughout the season, you'll constantly have to inform your players about matters such as schedule changes, postponed games, upcoming events, and important team news. Having a specific parent (or two) responsible for helping you make these calls will be a big help. Parents can also assist in organizing and running fundraisers, arranging carpools, and helping to chaperone occasional trips to the ice cream parlor or pizza shop after the game.

It's always a good idea to select one or two parents to act as assistant coaches to help you run drills during practice and assist you in developing player skills. During games, they can help set up equipment, keep playbook records, distribute water bottles during time outs, and monitor substitutions to help ensure equal playing time for all the kids. If you don't know your team parents well, be careful before asking for volunteers to fill this position. It's much wiser to get to know the parents first, making sure that they believe in and respect your coaching philosophy. Take the time to see how they interact with the kids as well as with the other parents. This will help you identify those moms or dads you feel may be well suited for the position—those who will support your teaching methods and who will emphasize fun and good sportsmanship. You don't want to select a seemingly laid-back dad as an assistant coach only to discover that he turns into a win-at-all-costs screaming lunatic once the games begin!

Some leagues may depend on parents to fill the role of referees or umpires, especially for starter teams like T-ball, peewee baseball, and introductory basketball and soccer. If your league does this, mention it at the meeting. Find out which parents would be willing to fill these positions if the need arises (some may be uncomfortable with these kinds of jobs and would rather not be asked). And don't wait until the last minute. You don't want to find yourself scrambling around moments before the game starts, looking for a parent to umpire third base or to serve as linesman for a soccer game.

Depending on the league and the needs of your particular team, other voluntary positions may be available. Whatever the tasks, encourage your team parents to get involved and lend a hand.

ALLOW TIME FOR QUESTIONS

Those in attendance will probably be asking you questions throughout the meeting. However, be sure to provide a question-and-answer period at the end of the meeting for any final questions or concerns of those in attendance. If there is any-

thing you are not able to answer, make note of it and get back
with the information as soon as possible.

Remember, a preseason parents meeting lays the ground-
work for a smooth-running season, opens the communications
link, and is integral in getting you and the parents pulling in
the same direction.

PREPARING FOR GAMES

Any good coach knows that showing up for a game a few
minutes before it starts is simply not an option. In addition to
planning out strategies and plays before arriving at the field or
court, there are a number of pregame responsibilities that
require your early presence.

As discussed in the inset "Offer Equal Opportunity" in
Chapter 2, prior to games, it's a good idea to prepare a list that
includes your lineup or starting players along with your sub-
stitution rotation. This will help ensure that everyone gets
an equal amount of playing time and is able to play a few different positions. If you don't take a few minutes to do this
prior to the game, you'll discover that once the game starts, it
will become difficult to keep track of how much time and
which position each child has played. Don't risk denying
some youngsters an equal amount of game action. Remember,
every child on your team signed up to play, not watch from
the bench.

Upon arriving at the field or court, inspect the playing
area for potential dangers. Outdoors, keep an eye out for hazards such as broken glass, uneven ground, loose rocks, and
raised sprinklers. Indoors, look for wet or slippery spots on
the court floor—anything that could cause an injury during the

course of play. Don't rely on the opposing coach or a grounds crew to do this. Every player participating in the game is your responsibility.

Once your players have arrived, gather them together for a pregame talk. Preferably, speak to them away from their parents and anything else that may distract them from what you have to say. Keep this meeting short and to the point—the fewer instructions the better. Don't get bogged down talking about strategy, and never introduce new plays that haven't been covered in practice. Go over the starting squad or lineup and make sure each player understands his or her responsibilities. It's okay to reinforce one or two major points that you've covered during practice, just don't overdo it. You don't want to overload the kids with information. There's no need for any "Win one for the Gipper" speeches either. Simply maintain a relaxed demeanor and speak in an even tone. If you appear nervous or uptight, your players are likely to feel that way, too, and it will infringe on their ability to play the game. Be sure to stress that you want everyone to have fun and display good sportsmanship—win or lose. Let them know the most important thing is that they do their best. Make sure everyone has the necessary equipment, and then get them started on pregame warm-ups.

Before the game starts, head over to meet the opposing coach. This is a sign of good sportsmanship and sets a good example for the players on both teams, as well as their parents, siblings, and any other spectators. At this time, you'll mention or discover any players with special needs. Perhaps there is a child with a vision problem or hearing impairment that may require special consideration. If this is the case, discuss any necessary rule modifications that will ensure that child is able to enjoy the full benefits of participation. Before walking away, shake hands and wish the other coach a "good game."

Also introduce yourself to the officials. Let them know that you want to be informed if any of your players say or do anything that can be construed as unsportsmanlike behavior. This goes for any comments from parents or other spectators as well. Do everything you can to work *with* the officials, not against them.

PREVENTING AND DEALING WITH INJURIES

There's no getting around the fact that anyone who steps onto a playing field, no matter what age or skill level, is vulnerable to injury. While it is impossible to eliminate this threat altogether, you can greatly reduce the chances of your players getting injured during practices and games by following some basic safety guidelines:

⊛ Inspect the playing area for potential hazards. Check for glass, rocks, or litter on outdoor playing fields, as well as holes or ruts that can cause a player to trip. Also consider weather conditions. At the first sign of lightning, immediately get your players off the field. For indoor sports, check courts or tracks for wet areas, debris, or any foreign matter that could trigger a fall.

⊛ Make sure that each player is wearing the required equipment, which must also be the correct size and properly fitted. Insist on the use of any safety gear that is specific to the sport, such as helmets, mouth guards, kneepads, shin guards, elbow pads, and safety goggles.

⊛ Be sure the players are adequately conditioned and have

the basic skills necessary to play the sport or a particular position of that sport.

⚽ Always hold warm-up exercises before games and practices. Many injuries can be prevented if players are properly stretched and loosened up before engaging in the sport.

⚽ To avoid dehydration, encourage your players to drink plenty of liquids before games and practices, and at regular intervals during the activity. Make it a team rule for every child to carry a water bottle. It is also a good practice to keep a large "team" jug or thermos of water on hand at all times.

⚽ Make sure to give your players enough breaks during games and practices to rest and recharge. When players become tired and weak, they are more likely to play sloppily and make errors, which can result in injuries.

⚽ If any children on your team have medical conditions, such as asthma or diabetes, or have serious allergic reactions to insect bites or certain foods, be prepared to deal with any emergencies that may arise from these special circumstances.

Furthermore:

⚽ Know how to administer first aid for basic emergencies such as skin lacerations and bloody noses, as well as how to perform techniques such as CPR. Many organized youth leagues require emergency training for all of their coaches.

⚽ Always carry a properly equipped first aid kit to games and practices. It should include the following basic items: latex gloves (to wear when administering to bloody wounds); pre-moistened towelettes (for cleaning cuts and scrapes); alcohol swabs; antibiotic cream; adhesive bandages (in assorted sizes); athletic tape; gauze pads (in various sizes); tea bags (when moistened with water, these help stop bleeding in the mouth); an Ace bandage; scissors; nail clippers; tweezers; and a small flashlight (for checking pupils in case of a possible concussion). In addition, always have an ice pack or two on hand— the type that is activated when smacked against a hard surface. And in the event you have to administer CPR, keep a mouth guard among your emergency supplies to help protect against the oral transmission of disease.

⚽ Do not administer any oral medication.

⚽ Try to have access to a cell phone in the event of an emergency. If not, be sure to know the location of the nearest public telephone.

⚽ Never allow an injured player to "play through the pain."

⚽ If a player sustains an injury that requires a doctor's attention, do not allow the child to return to play until you have received written consent from the doctor.

⚽ Always proceed with caution when dealing with an injury, but be particularly careful with those involving the head, neck, and/or spine. Never attempt to move a player who is lying on the ground with such an injury. Doing so is likely to cause further damage.

In addition to the guidelines presented above, remember that cultivating an atmosphere of healthy competition and personal growth while encouraging a positive self-image can do more to help your players avoid injuries than a "get out there and win" attitude. Young athletes who are expected to win at all costs are more likely to sustain injuries while trying to meet unrealistic expectations. And remember, not all injuries are physical. Always support your players' efforts no matter what the score, and encourage parents and other spectators to do the same.

SUMMING IT UP

Being well prepared can contribute greatly to your overall effectiveness as a coach. In large part, your ability to ensure that everyone has an enjoyable season hinges on it. So take the time to develop a well thought out coaching philosophy and then live by it, outline the upcoming season for the parents in a special meeting, and come to each game prepared to encourage an atmosphere in which each player on the team will experience fun and enjoyment.

5. DEALING WITH PROBLEMS

Today's youth sports climate is more intense and volatile than ever before. Increasing numbers of parents, players, and coaches alike are displaying poor sportsmanship, disrespect, and rage at games. Ideally, every child who laces up skates, straps on shin guards, or dons a pair of shoulder pads should enjoy a positive and enriching youth sports experience without the burden of witnessing such negative behavior. Most of them do. However, the threat of inappropriate, sometimes dangerous conduct continues to cast dark shadows over far too many organized sports programs.

Typically, it is the adults—spectators as well as coaches—who are the major source of improper conduct seen at games. Most commonly, this misbehavior involves hurtful or callous remarks to players, game officials, and/or each other, as well as inappropriate, often vulgar gestures. Occasionally, what may start out as an insensitive remark can escalate into a more serious confrontation—pushing, shoving, fistfighting, and even full-scale brawling. Not only does such behavior put the combatants themselves (and bystanders) at physical risk, it also sends a negative message to the children, who are either participating in the game or watching from the sidelines. Of course, it is not only the adults who display poor behavior. Don't count out disruptive incidents by the young players themselves.

As a good coach, your job is to be aware of what to expect, and then have a plan for dealing with any questionable behavior that might arise. This chapter, therefore, will help prepare you for *conflict resolution*—dealing with negative situations, both large and small, efficiently and effectively. It also presents ways to diffuse potential problems before they have had a chance to manifest.

Being able to deal with all types of conflicts—no matter how serious or seemingly insignificant—is a vital skill for any volunteer coach. And although you may never face any of the problems presented in this chapter, you should still be aware that they exist and have a plan for dealing with them should they occur. As mentioned in the previous chapter, always be prepared. This becomes especially important during tense situations during which the approach you take can make the difference between diffusing a potentially explosive occurrence or merely adding to its volatility.

So, let's take a look at some of the most common problem areas and discuss ways in which you can effectively deal with them should the need arise.

PROBLEMS WITH YOUR PLAYERS

Potential problems involving your young players can encompass a wide range of negative behaviors—some more serious than others. For instance, you may have to deal with youngsters who are lax when it comes to following directions—you know, the ones who always show up late for games or practices and never seem to bring the required equipment. Others may be disrespectful of your authority as a coach and rebel against your rules, no matter what they are. Some players may be overly aggressive around their teammates, bullying some and challenging others. There may be players on your team who have a propensity for using foul language, while others are simply poor sports. The good news is that most of these behaviors are manageable, especially if they are dealt with at the first sign of trouble. It's your job to address these behaviors before they evolve into anything severe.

As the coach, you always hold the trump card—playing time. This is a very powerful incentive. The threat of sitting on the bench or sidelines for any period of time is usually enough of a punishment to warrant a turnaround in a child's behavior. But don't spring this or any other form of discipline on your players without warning. Do yourself a huge favor—at the beginning of the season, outline your ground rules to the team. Be very clear, very specific about the behaviors you consider unacceptable. And be sure to let the kids know the possible ramifications for these behaviors.

Many coaches find the "three-strikes" technique to be an effective approach when dealing with *most* infractions. With it, the first time a child displays a form of unacceptable behavior, he or she is given a verbal warning, which is considered "strike one." The child is also made aware that a stricter measure will be taken if the infraction occurs again, and it is critical to tell the child what that measure will be. Many coaches find that having the player sit out of the game for a number of minutes (or a period, half, or inning) is appropriate. When enforcing "strike two," be sure to make the child aware of the discipline he or she will face if "strike three" occurs. Elimination of playing time for an undetermined period is usually very effective. The child must understand the inappropriateness of his or her action, and realize how it infringes on the rest of the team. You might also consider having the child apologize to the other players.

When a gradual system of punishment, such as the "three-strikes" method, is enforced, and playing time is at risk, most youngsters won't even venture into first-strike territory. And those individuals who do will rarely go further. Ideally, most of the kids will realize that they have stepped across the boundary of good behavior and, with playing time at stake, will usually conform.

To be most effective as a coach, there are a few additional considerations to keep in mind when dealing with behavioral problems. First, do not use conditioning drills as a form of punishment. Disciplining unacceptable behavior by having a child run laps or do pushups is counterproductive. Conditioning plays an important role in most sports; using it as punishment will give it a negative spin—something you never want to do.

Another important rule—be sure to follow through with any disciplinary measures you have set. Be true to your word. If you have promised a certain punishment for a particular inappropriate action, don't back down if an infraction occurs. The kids on your team must know that you are serious about what you say. If you don't follow through, you'll lose credibility, making it difficult to gain their trust and respect during the season.

To establish consistency and a sense of fairness, be sure that your behavioral rules apply to everyone. Don't play favorites, and never make a separate set of rules for players with different playing abilities. Doing so will cause disruption and resentment among the players. And always make sure the "punishment fits the crime." The disciplinary measure for a child who constantly forgets to bring his glove to games shouldn't be the same one used for the player who curses at the umpire or punches another player in the nose.

PROBLEMS WITH OPPOSING COACHES

There's just no getting around the fact that you're going to run into coaches who simply don't get it when it comes to youth sports. They're the ones you'll see pacing up and down the field or court, yelling and screaming at their young players in an effort to imitate the coaches of their favorite professional teams. They're also the ones who rage against game officials, deriding and intimidating them when calls don't go their way. They are the coaches who perceive the games as life-and-death affairs, and do everything within their power to come out on the winning end. They forge ahead with their teams as if they're participating in the Super Bowl, World Series, NBA Championship, and World Cup all rolled into one.

The best way to combat rude, obnoxious coaches in front

Time Out! for Better Sports for Kids

The Time Out! for Better Sports for Kids initiative was created by NAYS to help extinguish the increasing amount of negative behavior displayed at youth sporting events. The program's goal is to ensure a safe environment for children, their parents and other spectators, coaches, and officials. Headed by Olympic track champion Marion Jones, this public service campaign brings concerned citizens together with their local recreation departments to effect positive changes in how their youth sports programs are conducted. For more information, or to obtain a free copy of the program's informative video, call 1-800-729-2057 or visit www.timeoutforbettersportsforkids.org.

of your players and any spectators is through your own model behavior. Keep a level head when others around you are losing theirs. Stay focused on your coaching philosophy, which should always have the best interest of the children at heart. Remember, all eyes will be on you; the kids will take their cues from you and the way you act.

But what if the opposing coach's win-at-all-costs rude behavior escalates into using foul language? Don't ignore it! Swearing has absolutely no place in youth sports. When words are laced with curses and obscenities, it's time for you to take an active step in putting a stop to this behavior. Immediately point out the inappropriateness of the coach's offensive banter to either the game official or a league supervisor, who should be in attendance at the game. After all, children are listening. Prompt the official to remind the coach that this type of language will not be tolerated. (The same rule applies to parents and other spectators who are guilty of using foul language.) In most leagues, if the offending coach continues to speak inappropriately, the official will issue a warning, stating that the continued use of this language will result in his or her forfeiting the game. In most instances, once an official has issued the threat of a forfeit, the coach will immediately clean up the offensive language. Although you may not want to play the role of an antagonist in this type of situation, it's important that you do. Make it clear that you will not allow your team to participate in this type of environment.

Even more serious is facing a situation that involves a coach (or any other adult for that matter) who gets physically abusive during games. And this abuse can be directed at anyone—you, the parents, or the players on either team. As soon as a coach's words or body language reaches a confrontational level and the threat of physical violence is imminent, most game officials will stop play in an attempt to diffuse the obvious problem. And if the official doesn't stop the game, you should cease playing anyway. No contest is ever worth risking your well-being, or that of your players or their parents.

Don't ever take threatening behavior lightly. And when tempers flare, don't expect the heightened tension to subside quickly. Matter of fact, it is more likely to escalate. All it takes is one riled-up coach to ignite the parents of his players, who are likely to join in the altercation with a barrage of angry words and, in extreme cases, a physical exchange—often with each other. Nothing can mar a child more than witnessing a fight among adults, particularly parents and coaches. It's something no child should have to experience. And this type of conduct can and does occur at games of all levels, including T-ball, peewee ball, and other early-level teams. No sport is immune, and certainly no community is either.

If you believe any situation appears to be on the brink of certain physical confrontation, call the authorities immediately. It's usually best to get your kids off the field and gather all the parents around. And if, in fact, a physical outbreak does occur, do everything in your power to keep the parents of your players from getting involved; it will only add fuel to a growing fire. Once a fight starts and punches are thrown, everyone is accountable for his or her behavior. Everyone shares the blame, regardless of who actually started the altercation. You don't want to see your team on the evening news.

PROBLEMS WITH PARENTS

Parents or guardians of your players are an extension of you and your team. As a result, dealing with those who exhibit problematic behavior is somewhat manageable and often preventable. If you have held a preseason parents meeting, as suggested in Chapter 4, you have already taken an important preventive measure in avoiding bad behavior. At this meeting, you should have presented your behavioral ground rules, which outline the conduct you consider acceptable from both them and their children.

If one of your parents displays inappropriate conduct, address it immediately. For instance, if you hear a parent direct a vicious or mean-spirited comment toward a player, game official, or opposing coach, don't ignore it. As soon as possible, let the parent know that the comment is not acceptable— that it is not in keeping with the positive spirit and good sportsmanship that you are striving to achieve with the team. Ignoring this behavior will send the wrong message and open the door for other parents to behave in the same way. However, taking a stand will reinforce the message that this type of behavior will not be tolerated.

In most instances, a stern lecture isn't necessary. Some offenders may not even realize what they are doing and a gentle reminder to monitor their actions or language more closely may be all that is warranted. Sometimes, simply making eye contact and shaking your head in a nonapproving way is enough to make the point. However, if the misconduct continues, a more forceful approach may be in order. Let the offenders know, in clear terms, that they *must* regain their composure and be in control of their behavior. Make them see that they are a distraction to the players as well as the other spectators.

Most leagues give umpires, referees, and other game officials permission to ban offending spectators (as well as coaches and players) from games. Some leagues allow coaches this same power. If your league is one of them, be sure that you are aware of all the steps that must be followed before having a spectator removed from a game. And although you may have this authority, it is always best to do everything in your power to avoid exercising it. Banning parents from games is an extreme measure that is never encouraged. It is an embarrassment for both the parent and the child, who has to bear witness to the parental reprimand in front of friends and teammates. If, however, you are put into a position in which you have no choice but to instruct a parent to leave, try to do so discreetly.

Parents play an integral role in the entire youth sports process, and it's best to use measures that don't eliminate them from the picture. A number of leagues have implemented ways of dealing with poor parental conduct. For example, some have started "Silent Saturdays," which ban all parents in attendance from making *any* comments—good or bad—during the games. Although this allows all of the parents to attend games, it is not conducive to a fun and enjoyable environment. The misbehavior of a few parents robs the majority from offering positive encouragement. There is no rooting for the team or cheering for good plays. This type of environment is certainly not what youth sports is all about.

Altering the score as a penalty for bad behavior is another method of discipline utilized by some leagues. If a parent misbehaves, a specified number of points are deducted from their team's score. Although this can be an effective approach for maintaining order and civility in the stands, it is certainly not fair to the players.

Most disturbing is that a number of leagues have simply been forced to shut down due to dangerous behavior displayed during games. Some leagues that experience similar behavior problems have resorted to hiring police officers to maintain order both in the stands and on the playing field. The cost of this service is worked into the registration fee. Although this may be an extreme measure and a sad commentary on our society, at least it allows the children to participate within a safe environment.

The good news is that the majority of your parents are likely to be well behaved, especially if they know what you expect from them. Keep the lines of communication open, and always be on guard to diffuse any problems before they have had a chance to develop.

SUMMING IT UP

There's no room in youth sports for bad behavior—not from the players, the spectators, or from other coaches. Hopefully, you will never be forced to discipline a child on your team, deal with a foul-mouthed coach, or witness a physical confrontation between parents.

In the event, however, that a problematic situation or conflict does arise, as the coach, it is your responsibility to act swiftly and fairly to resolve the matter and restore order. Turning your back on an obvious problem is not the answer. And don't expect someone else to take care of it—you are responsible for at least trying to set the matter straight.

Remember you're the coach, and with the job come responsibilities. Always serve as a role model, exhibiting good sportsmanship and a sense of fair play. Strive to maintain an enjoyable environment that encourages fun while supporting the needs, skills, and all-around best interests of the children. Stick to these basic guidelines and you'll meet with success!

CONCLUSION

As a volunteer coach, you are about to embark on a wonderful journey. After reading this book, you are well aware of the importance of this role and the enormous influence it has on everyone connected with the team, especially the children.

You've learned that as a top-quality coach, your primary mission should always be to lead your team through an enjoyable season of healthy competition and good sportsmanship within a stress-free, fun-filled environment. You've also seen how this role extends way beyond teaching players how to field grounders or sink jump shots. It's all about the emotional bond you'll form with the kids as you watch them grow and develop during the course of the season. It's about teaching them through your good example. It's also about the gigantic smiles they'll flash upon hearing your words of praise and encouragement, the sparkle in their eyes when they've mastered a new skill, the friendships you'll form with some of the parents, the special connections you'll develop with certain players, and the fun-filled post-game parties that everyone will remember for years to come. In addition to building a child's physical skill development, youth sports also has the wonderful capability of bolstering a child's confidence, self-esteem, and social skills—positive attributes that will be carried into adulthood. And lucky you, you're going to play a major role in nurturing this development.

Although this book may have illustrated more coaching responsibilities than you realized when you signed up for the job, don't be overwhelmed by them. Never doubt your ability to fill this role for even a second. You're going to do a wonderful job, and we applaud you for volunteering. We also commend you for taking the time to read this book and learn the responsibilities of this role—it shows that you care. Through proper preparation and by working together with other adults involved in the program, you can sidestep conflict, create a positive atmosphere, and help ensure a rewarding experience for everyone involved.

Remember, your team's win-loss record isn't an accurate gauge of your coaching abilities. If the children under your care learn and develop skills—and have fun in the process— the shiniest trophy will pale in comparison! Thank you for volunteering and for taking the time to properly prepare for this very special job.

Good luck this season.

National
ALLIANCE
For Youth Sports

The National Alliance For Youth Sports (NAYS) is America's leading advocate for positive and safe sports for children. The Alliance features a wide range of programs to educate volunteer coaches, parents, game officials, and youth sport program administrators about their roles and responsibilities in the context of youth sports.

In addition, the Alliance offers youth development programs for children. The programs are provided at the local level through dynamic partnerships with more than 2,400 community-based organizations, such as parks and recreation departments, Boys and Girls Clubs, Police Athletic Leagues, YMCA/YWCAs, and other independent youth service groups throughout the country and military installations worldwide.

For further information on the Alliance or any of its programs, call them toll-free at 1-800-688-KIDS or visit the NAYS website at www.nays.org.

INDEX